Amazing Nature

Marvellous Migrators

Tim Knight

www.heinemann.co.uk/library
Visit our website to find out more information about **Heinemann Library** books.

To order:
- Phone 44 (0) 1865 888066
- Send a fax to 44 (0) 1865 314091
- Visit the Heinemann Bookshop at www.heinemann.co.uk/library to browse our catalogue and order online.

First published in Great Britain by Heinemann Library, Halley Court, Jordan Hill, Oxford OX2 8EJ, part of Harcourt Education.
Heinemann is a registered trademark of Harcourt Education Ltd.

© Harcourt Education Ltd 2003
First published in paperback in 2005
The moral right of the proprietor has been asserted.

All rights reserved. No part of this publication may be reproduced, stored in a retrieval system, or transmitted in any form or by any means, electronic, mechanical, photocopying, recording, or otherwise, without either the prior written permission of the publishers or a licence permitting restricted copying in the United Kingdom issued by the Copyright Licensing Agency Ltd, 90 Tottenham Court Road, London W1T 4LP (www.cla.co.uk).

Editorial: Jilly Attwood and Claire Throp
Design: David Poole and Geoff Ward
Picture Research: Peter Morris
Production: Séverine Ribierre

Originated by Ambassador Litho Ltd
Printed and bound in Hong Kong, China by South China Printing Company

ISBN 0 431 16653 6 (hardback)
07 06 05 04 03
10 9 8 7 6 5 4 3 2 1

ISBN 0 431 16658 7 (paperback)
08 07 06 05
10 9 8 7 6 5 4 3 2 1

British Library Cataloguing in Publication Data
Knight, Tim
Marvellous Migrators - (Amazing Nature)
535.6
A full catalogue record for this book is available from the British Library.

Acknowledgements
The Publishers would like to thank the following for permission to reproduce photographs:
Ardea p. **21**; Bruce Coleman pp. **15**, **22**; Bruce Coleman pp. **5** (Jorg and Petra Wegner), **6** (Dr Eckart Pott), **11** (Pacific Stock), **13** (Gunter Ziesler), **20** (Fred Bruemmer); Corbis p. **25** (Wayne Lawler); FLPA pp. **8** (E & D Hosking), **9** (Steve Maslowski), **14** (Mark Newman), **18** (Terry Whittaker), **19** (P David), **26** (Roger Tidman); Heather Angel p. **7**; NHPA pp. **4** (Stephen Dalton), **10** (Bill Coster), **12** (Jeff Goodman), **16-17** (B & C Alexander), **23** (Martin Harvey), **24** (Hellio and Van Ingen), **27** (Anthony Bannister)

Cover photograph of Monarch butterflies, reproduced with permission of Nature Picture Library/Tom Mangelsen.

Every effort has been made to contact copyright holders of any material reproduced in this book. Any omissions will be rectified in subsequent printings if notice is given to the Publishers.

GLOUCESTERSHIRE COUNTY LIBRARY	
9932709069	
PETERS	20-Feb-2009
591.568	£7.75

Contents

Mobile homes	4
Travelling light	6
Free as a bird	8
Powered flight	10
Long distance walkers	12
Journeys under the sea	14
River adventure	16
Fish out of water	18
Annual visits	20
The wanderers	22
Alien invasion	24
Finding the way	26
Fact file	28
Glossary	30
Index	32

Any words appearing in the text in bold, **like this**, are explained in the Glossary.

mobile homes

Some animals spend their entire lives in the same place. This area is known as a **habitat**. Others move to a new habitat at least once during their lifetime, or live in different places at different times of the year.

These movements to a new home are known as migration. Some animals migrate in search of food or water. Others seek shelter or somewhere safe to raise a family. Some move to escape the cold, some to avoid the heat.

Most types of migration are regular events. For example, every autumn millions of birds in North America fly south. The food supply of **nectar**, insects and meat becomes harder to find at this time of year, so the birds fly to where food is more plentiful. Every spring, the same birds make the return journey to their **breeding grounds** in the north. In Europe, many birds also fly south to escape the cold northern winter.

Twice a year, millions of European swallows migrate to and from South Africa across the Mediterranean Sea and the Sahara Desert.

Other movements do not follow any pattern. Severe **drought**, heavy rain, an increase in population, or an unexpected change in temperature may be all it can take to trigger a sudden large movement of animals.

Scientists are still discovering new facts about the incredible journeys that some animals make. The story of animal migration is a remarkable tale, full of amazing facts and unsolved mysteries.

At the start of the rainy season, herds of zebra leave the dry, dusty plain and head for the places where the first new grass is beginning to grow.

Travelling light

Most insects look too lightweight and flimsy to fly long distances, but appearances can be **deceptive**. While some butterflies never move far from the place where they hatched, others travel thousands of kilometres.

The North American monarch is the most famous migrating butterfly. Every autumn, hundreds of millions of monarchs fly up to 4000 kilometres to escape the cold winter. Each new generation of butterflies follows exactly the same route. Stopping only to rest for the night, they can cover over 100 kilometres in a single day. Their journey south ends in Mexico. Here they **hibernate** in vast numbers in a few favourite valleys. In spring they fly north again. This time they move more slowly. They feed and breed along the way. Most of them die before reaching their original home.

Hibernating monarch butterflies cling to the tree branches, clustering together to keep warm.

Large numbers of newly hatched bogong moths escape the heat of summer by retreating into Australia's highest mountain range. There they crawl into dark, cool cracks in the rocks. The shelters become so overcrowded that thousands of moths spill out around the edges.

Young spiders migrate too. They have no wings, so they hitch a ride to new feeding grounds by turning themselves into tiny kites. They cling to fine threads of their own silk. The threads and spider are swept into the air and carried away on the breeze. Using air **currents** in this way is known as 'ballooning'.

The overlapping bodies of bogong moths crowd into a shady spot high in the Australian Alps.

7

Free as a bird

Birds are able to travel long distances. English swallows cross the burning Sahara Desert to their winter home in South Africa. On their autumn migration to India, bar-headed geese from Tibet, and demoiselle cranes from Siberia, have to fly incredibly high. To cross the Himalayas, the highest mountains in the world, they fly at heights of over 5500 metres.

Arctic terns make a return trip to Antarctica every year. They divide their time between the North and South Poles. Arctic terns enjoy two summers in a row by leaving each pole just before the dark winter sets in. With 24-hour sunshine throughout the year, the Arctic tern sees more daylight than any other animal on Earth.

An Arctic tern may break its marathon journey from pole to pole by resting on the sea or perching on icebergs.

The mighty atom
For sheer determination, the migration of the ruby-throated hummingbird takes some beating. It migrates from Canada to Panama in Central America, and back again. The tiny bird flies through North America, stopping off along the way to feed on flowers. The most direct route into Central America is straight across the Gulf of Mexico. However, the sea crossing is risky, even for large birds. The ruby-throated hummingbird weighs only a few grams, but flies straight across the 800 kilometres of open water. It risks everything on being able to do this non-stop 18-hour flight!

A migrating hummingbird on its long journey south pauses briefly to refuel in mid-air.

Powered flight

Long-distance flying uses up a lot of time and energy. Birds need to make sure that they have enough wing power for the journey.

In the few weeks before it migrates from Europe to South Africa, the sedge warbler doubles its weight from 11 to 22 grams. This gives it enough energy to fly for 90 hours without a rest. Sandpipers and other small wading birds also eat extra food before migration. Their brain and other organs shrink to make more room for the **fat reserves** that the birds need for the long journey ahead.

Heavy birds, such as geese, must fly quickly to stay in the air. This uses up lots of energy, so they need to break their journey many times to feed. They often fly during the night to keep cool.

Flocks of migrating geese, called skeins, fly in a 'v' formation. Each bird takes a turn at the front, while the rest of the flock fly in its slipstream.

Riding the wind

Birds of prey, such as eagles, hawks and buzzards, save energy by riding on **thermals**. These are **currents** of warm air that lift them high in the sky. They travel long distances by gliding slowly on the thermals. There are no thermals over the sea. Birds flying from Europe to Africa try to cross the Mediterranean at its narrowest point – the Straits of Gibraltar. Birds of prey normally live on their own, but at migration time they crowd together in vast numbers to cross the sea at the same place.

Bald eagles often migrate in large groups, spread out in a long stream up to 50 kilometres long.

Long distance walkers

Walking long distances takes much more time than flying, so most land animals avoid long migrations. Some animals have no choice – they have to migrate to survive. For example, animals will have to move if their food supply runs out or freezes over.

Caribou spend the summer feeding on moss and grass in the Arctic tundra. Before winter arrives, the herds head south, to look for food and shelter in the forests. The biggest herds contain nearly half a million animals. They travel up to 65 kilometres a day to escape the snow and freezing wind. As spring returns, they follow the same migration route back to their **breeding grounds**, nearly 1000 kilometres away in the far north.

*Emus cannot fly, but they walk further than any other bird. In times of **drought**, emus walk up to 480 kilometres across Australia in search of water.*

Migrating wildebeests struggle to climb the steep, muddy bank, blocking the escape route of the animals in the river behind them.

Plain travel

The largest herds of migrating animals are found on the plains of East Africa. The most famous is the wildebeest. Twice every year, a million wildebeests and 200,000 zebras migrate to the Serengeti plains. Their grassland home in Kenya begins to dry out, so they 'follow the rains' to greener grass in Tanzania. Their pounding hooves kick up a trail of dust stretching for miles across the plain.

At one point in their journey, the crocodile-infested Mara River blocks the wildebeests' path. There is a mad scramble to cross the flooded river. Many thousands of wildebeest are drowned, trampled underfoot, or killed by hungry predators. Six months later, the survivors make the same journey in reverse.

Journeys under the sea

In the deep ocean, marine animals are busy migrating, hidden from the eyes of the world. Scientists recently found out that northern elephant seals spend over half their lives migrating between California and the North Pacific. The return journey covers around 19,000 kilometres and is the longest known migration for a **mammal**.

Humpback whales sing to each other during their long migratory journeys. They travel from the waters where they breed to their winter feeding grounds. As they travel, their songs keep changing. Scientists have yet to discover the real reason for this.

Coming up for air. Because seals can swim long distances underwater, their migration routes are not easy to follow.

Lobster convoy

Spiny lobsters live in holes on coral reefs near the Bahamas. In autumn, at the first sign of stormy weather, they gather together on the sandy sea bottom. Here they form long columns of 50 or more and march off in single file across the seabed. The lobsters head for deeper water, where they will be safe from the storms. The deep water is much colder, which slows down the lobsters so that they use less energy. This helps them to survive at a time when there is not much food. If the lobsters are in danger, they form a tight circle, facing outwards. They fight off the enemy with their spiky antennae.

Sticking together for protection, spiny lobsters move across the sandy sea floor like a camel train across the desert.

River adventure

Migrating salmon have to make one of nature's toughest journeys. Salmon spend most of their life in the sea. When fully grown, they swim hundreds of kilometres back to the river where they were born.

In late summer, they swim back and begin to gather around the coast. Each salmon heads for the **estuary** that leads back to its birthplace. Reaching the coast is the easy bit. The real test comes when they begin to swim upriver.

The salmon have to battle against the strong **current**. They also have to fight their way past many obstacles. In Alaska, migrating Pacific salmon have to dodge hungry brown bears. The bears hang around the 'salmon leaps' waiting for an easy meal. In places, fierce rapids or high waterfalls block the salmon's path. They launch themselves out of the water by thrashing their tails.

A salmon may have to make many tiring leaps before it can finally land in the calmer water above the falls.

Once in a lifetime
Eventually, the salmon reach the stream where they were born, but there is no time for rest – they must fight for a mate, before they can begin to **breed**. A Pacific salmon only makes this incredible journey once in a lifetime. Every single fish dies after **spawning**. They are too exhausted to return to the sea. The following spring, all the eggs hatch. The tiny salmon, known as fry, swim back out to sea. A few years later the fully grown salmon will return to the same river on their final journey in life.

Fish out of water

Adult eels migrate huge distances when they are ready to **breed**. Many of these eels have grown up in European rivers. They leave these feeding grounds and swim thousands of kilometres to the Sargasso sea. This area of warm water in the western Atlantic is where all the eels lay their eggs.

The newly-hatched eels are called glass eels. They too have to make a long journey. The glass eels travel deep in the ocean, and are carried along by a strong **current** called the Gulf Stream. The entire journey takes about 18 months.

By the time they have reached the coast of Europe, they look like a tiny, see-through version of an adult eel. They head straight for the nearest **estuary** and swim upriver. The eels stay close to the banks, to keep away from the strong currents, which would sweep them back out to sea. To avoid waterfalls, they slither out of the water and wriggle up the slippery banks before returning to the river.

Newly-hatched eels look like long, thin, transparent leaves. As they cross the Atlantic, their bodies change shape.

Migrating elvers gather together in a slithering, squirming ball as their path upriver is blocked by a sluice gate.

The young eels, known as **elvers**, live in fresh water for several years. When they are old enough to breed, they make the long journey back to their birthplace. The eels rest during the heat of the day and travel mainly at night. They usually swim downriver to the sea, but they will crawl across damp fields if this is the quickest route back to the coast.

Once in the sea, the eels dive so deep that they disappear without a trace. Six months later, they reappear 5600 kilometres away in the Sargasso Sea. Here they **spawn** and die. How they get there nobody really knows.

Annual visits

Unlike eels and most salmon, which die as soon as they have **spawned**, some animals return to the same **breeding grounds** year after year.

Sea turtles spend most of their lives in the ocean, but they have to migrate back to the land to lay their eggs. Every **breeding season**, the females swim to the same stretch of sandy beach as the year before. There are only a few safe beaches left in the world, so the turtles do not have much choice in where to nest. On some of the most overcrowded beaches, turtles arrive in such numbers that they have to climb over each other to find a space. In Costa Rica, more than 100,000 olive Ridley turtles have been counted on a single beach.

A female olive Ridley turtle drags her heavy body ashore.

A scarlet tide of baby Christmas Island crabs floods past an adult and heads for the safety of the forest.

Land crabs visit the sea to **spawn**. Every year on Christmas Island, a speck of land in the Indian Ocean, an amazing mass migration happens. The island's red crabs start to migrate as soon as the **monsoon** rains begin. In the rain, the crabs are safe from the burning tropical sun. Around 120 million red crabs leave their forest burrows and scuttle down to the seashore. Their migration march cuts straight across roads and gardens, making it impossible to drive or walk anywhere on the island without crushing crabs.

The wanderers

Some animals spend their whole lives on the move. They stop wherever they find a meal. They move on again as soon as the food runs out. This kind of movement follows no regular pattern, and is known as **nomadic migration**.

In the baking hot Australian desert, heavy rain may not fall for many years. When it finally arrives, it fills the dried-up lakes and rivers with water. Migrant ducks appear from nowhere. **Dormant** seeds quickly spring to life, covering the bare ground with flowering plants. Flocks of budgerigars and other seed-eating parrots also migrate into the area to take advantage of the feast.

In very severe winters, large flocks of waxwings fly across the North Sea from Scandinavia. They invade English gardens and strip the red berries from pyracantha and cotoneaster bushes. These sudden invasions, known as **irruptions**, only happen when their normal food supply runs out.

The nomadic budgerigar gathers in flocks wherever desert plants burst into flower.

When a massive flock of red-billed queleas drops in for a meal, the results are disastrous.

Birds of a feather

Nomadic migrants are not always welcome. The red-billed quelea, a seed-eating finch, gathers in enormous flocks of over a million birds. They will travel up to 1000 kilometres in search of food. A quelea flock in flight looks like a huge swarm of insects. Normally, queleas feed on wild grass seed, but if their natural food supply runs out, they may invade farmland. A million queleas can strip bare an entire field of wheat in minutes.

Alien invasion

Every few years, some animals, especially insects, have a 'bumper' **breeding season**. They produce so many **offspring** that there is not enough food to go round. The new generation has to move to a different area in search of food and a new home. This is known as **removal migration**. In many cases, the new arrivals become serious pests.

Desert locusts are one of the most unwelcome visitors. They normally live in the driest parts of North Africa, but now and again they breed in huge numbers and migrate to other parts of the world. They destroy crops along the way. During the worst locust **plagues**, a migrating swarm can spread out over an area of more than 28 million square kilometres.

Locusts regularly fly across the Red Sea, a distance of over 300 kilometres.

'Armyworm' is the name given to the migrating caterpillars that sweep across farmland all around the world. They move like an invading army, eating every bit of green vegetation in their path. The invasions, known as **infestations**, usually occur after a period of cold, wet weather. This is when armyworm enemies such as **parasites**, **predators** and disease are less common. Infestations soon spread to new areas because armyworm moths can travel over 100 kilometres in a single night.

Since they were brought to Australia, cane toads have spread through the country like a plague.

Stowaways

Migrating pests sometimes get a helping hand. Humans have a bad habit of introducing destructive animals into areas where they don't belong. By stowing away on boats, black rats have succeeded in reaching almost every part of the planet. Unwelcome invaders, such as black rats and cane toads, often drive out **native species** and take over their **habitat**.

Finding the way

How do all these long distance travellers find their way around? Tiny spiders and the weakest insects rely on luck. They end up wherever the breeze carries them. Some birds follow **geographical features**, such as coastlines, valleys and mountains. Other birds work out where they are from the position of the Sun. Those that fly by night use the stars to find their way instead. We know this because birds often fly off course when the sky is cloudy.

Insects also navigate by the Sun. Because the Sun's position in the sky keeps changing, the migration route of most butterflies varies according to what time of day they fly. All monarch butterflies, though, follow exactly the same route, whatever the time of day. They migrate in a straight line, guided by magnetic particles in their bodies.

*Migrating in bright sunshine, a flock of storks rides the **thermals** while following the landmarks below.*

Loggerhead turtles are born with a migration 'map' inside their heads. As soon as they hatch, baby loggerheads head for the sea. Mysteriously guided by the Earth's **magnetic field**, they start on a 13,000-kilometre 'swimathon' that may take 10 years to complete. They travel alone, following the same migration route used by their parents. Even scientists cannot explain exactly how it is done.

Fact file

The longest journey of all is made by the Arctic tern. Every year it flies non-stop to the Antarctic, a distance of over 19,000 kilometres.

In 1988, a massive swarm of desert locusts flew across the Atlantic from West Africa to the Caribbean. The 5000-kilometre crossing took 10 days and is the longest recorded insect migration.

Wading birds migrating from Scandinavia to the UK have been picked up on radar screens flying 7000 metres high.

Before they were massacred by settlers, 30 million bison used to migrate across the prairies of North America every autumn in search of fresh grass. Their hooves wore tracks so deep and wide that humans were able to use them as roads.

Manatees prefer to live in warm water and are more likely to catch diseases if they become too cold. In winter, if the water temperature falls below 68 degrees, they migrate to warmer areas such as natural springs, or places where power plants pump out heated waste water.

The world's oldest known living wild bird, a 50-year-old Manx shearwater, has probably migrated further than any other animal during its lifetime. Every year it makes a 16,000-kilometre round trip from Wales to Argentina, then back to the UK via North America. Its migration flights add up to 800,000 kilometres, the equivalent of flying 20 times round the Earth. Its total mileage, including feeding trips, adds up to an incredible 8 million kilometres, which is like flying to the Moon and back ten times.

When migrating swans are ready to take off, they need to let the whole flock know. The trumpeter swan bobs its head and neck up and down, and makes a clarion trumpet call.

Every summer, 20 million female free-tailed bats leave their home in Mexico and migrate north, without their mates. They all head for the same cave in Texas, almost 1000 miles away. Bracken Cave is where the bats give birth, but nobody knows why the females use it as a nursery year after year, especially when it is so far from home.

A salmon remembers the exact taste of the river where it was born. Even in the deep ocean, its super-sensitive nostrils pick up the scent of its home hundreds of miles away. When it is ready to breed, the salmon 'follows its nose' all the way back to its birthplace.

Glossary

breed to produce eggs or young

breeding grounds places where animals mate and raise their young

breeding season time of year when animals find a mate

current flowing water or air

deceptive misleading; hiding the truth

dormant non-active

drought long period without rain

elver young eel

estuary stretch of water where a river flows into the sea

fat reserves extra energy stored in the body, allowing an animal to survive for long periods without food

geographical features natural landmarks that are big enough to be seen from a distance

habitat place where an animal or plant lives

hibernate to sleep through the winter

infestation attack by a large number of pests, such as caterpillars

irruption sudden, unexpected invasion

magnetic field force around the Earth that pulls magnetic objects in a certain direction

mammal animal that feeds its young on milk from the mother's breast

monsoon seasonal wind that brings a long period of heavy rain

native species type of plant or animal that has always been found in a particular country, and was not taken there by people

nectar sugary liquid produced by flowers to attract insects

nomadic migration irregular movement in search of food

offspring children

parasite plant or animal that feeds on another living plant or animal

plague outbreak of pests or disease that spreads over a large area

predator animal that hunts and kills other living creatures

removal migration movement to avoid overcrowding or starvation

salmon run annual movement of salmon from the sea to the river

spawn to lay a mass of eggs in water

thermal rising current of warm air

Index

Arctic terns 8, 28
armyworm 25

ballooning 7
bats 29
birds 4, 8–11, 12, 22–3, 26, 28, 29
birds of prey 11
bison 28
breeding grounds 4, 12, 17, 18, 20
butterflies 6, 26

caribou 12
crabs 21

eels 18–19, 28
emus 12

fat reserves 10
food supplies 4, 9, 12, 22

geese 8, 10

habitat 4
hummingbirds 9

infestations 25
insects 6–7, 24, 26, 28
irruptions 22

land animals 12–13
lobsters 15
locusts 24, 28

marine animals 14–15
moths 7, 25

navigation 26–7
nomadic migration 22–3

pests 23, 24–5

queleas 23

rats 25
reasons for migration 4, 5
removal migration 24–5

salmon 16–17, 29
seals 14, 28
spawning 17, 19, 21
spiders 7, 26
stowaways 25
swallows 4, 8

territory 4
thermals 11, 26
turtles 20, 27

whales 14
wildebeest 13

zebras 5, 13